GROW NATIVE

GROW NATIVE

Landscaping with Native and Apt Plants of the Rocky Mountains

S. HUDDLESTON
M. HUSSEY

FULCRUM PUBLISHING
GOLDEN, COLORADO

Cover image by Bob Coonts

Cover design by Alyssa Pumphrey
Interior design by Jay Staten

Library of Congress Cataloging-in-Publication Data
Huddleston, S. (Sam)
    Grow native : landscaping with native and apt plants of the Rocky Mountains / by S. Huddleston, M. Hussey.
        p.   cm.
    Includes index.
    ISBN 1-55591-373-3 (pbk.)
    1. Native plant gardening—Rocky Mountains. 2. Landscape gardening—Rocky Mountains. 3. Native plants for cultivation—Rocky Mountains. 4. Plants, Ornamental—Rocky Mountains. I. Hussey, M. (Michael) II. Title.
SB439.24.R63H83   1998
635.9'5178—dc21   97-38574
                                                           CIP

Printed in United States of America

0 9 8 7 6 5 4 3 2 1

Fulcrum Publishing
350 Indiana Street, Suite 350
Golden, Colorado 80401-5093
(800) 992-2908 • (303) 277-1623
e-mail: fulcrum@fulcrum-gardening.com
website: www.fulcrum-gardening.com

A professional says of Grow Native:

This wonderful little book is approaching its fourth printing; its size belies the rich contents packed into the 96 pages. The authors lead the reader into the topic of plants with a discussion of the environmental conditions of the region and a brief presentation of landscape nomenclature.

The bulk of the book presents 50 trees, shrubs, ground covers, and grasses, with black-and-white photographs and descriptive text. Huddleston and Hussey have organized their information on each plant, and presented it briefly and succinctly. Plants are introduced by scientific and common names and are briefly described to the reader using the following topic outline: Suggested Uses, Planting Space, Height, Water, Exposure, and Suitable Substitutes.

Basic landscape design principles, planting instructions, water conservation tips, and a matrix chart (a quick cross-reference for plants, uses, tolerances, features, type, water requirements, and the page where the plant is listed) are included to help the Rocky Mountain gardener successfully grow these native plants.

Ken Ball
Member American Society of Landscape Architects (ASLA)
Registered Landscape Architect (RLA)
Founding Member, Xeriscape

CONTENTS

ACKNOWLEDGMENTS

We wish to thank Ken Ball of Xeriscape and Denver Water for his continued enthusiastic support toward the success of *Grow Native*.

Also, for particulars on Buffalograss we owe special thanks to John Pinder, manager, Little Valley Nurseries, Inc.

INTRODUCTION:

Major Environmental Influences on Plants of the Rocky Mountain Foothills

We hope this book will be of use to the owner, builder, and developer—you who relate your home and landscape to the very different environment of the foothills region, the east face of the Rockies in Colorado, northern New Mexico, and southern Wyoming, in the elevation range from 4,500 to 7,000 feet. Landscape architects, conservationists, environmentalists, and others concerned with the use of land will find the information herein of interest. Throughout the world there are similar locales where the book's content will be applicable.

The adaptation of native plants to the cultured landscapes of humans is not only practical in a horticultural sense but, perhaps most importantly, it is an expression by humans of their appreciation of nature and their desire to be in harmony with it.

Not every plant that grows wild in the foothills is included here. We have limited the list to representatives of the whole spectrum that are suitable for the ordinary landscape. Also listed are some important "foreigners" that adapt easily and are aesthetically appropriate. Some of these, such as the Russian Olive, have in fact "gone native."

While all plants require some care to achieve good results, we have restricted the list to those that are the most carefree and that can endure the blows that nature will inflict on them from time to time in the storms that roar out of the high country. To plants, the foothills pose a great range of growing conditions that include not only climate—available moisture, exposure to sun and wind—but also altitude (elevation) and soil variations from rock to peat bog. These microclimates and innumerable small ecosystems result in practically endless localized situations. For example, because of more sunshine and less exposure to cold winds, plants on the south side of a mountain will grow at a much higher elevation than the plants on the north side.

Let us look at the foothills climate. The same condition that results in severe sunburn in humans—extended exposure to infrared rays at a high altitude—probably has more influence on plant growth than any other factor. Only the natives take it well. Only the natives can live with our normal 10 to 20 inches allotment of moisture per year—trees native to the Midwest require *at least* 30 inches. Remember that moisture of either rain or snow increases with altitude. We observe that precipitation in the foothills generally ranges from about 14 inches at 4,500 feet above sea level to around 19 inches at 7,000 feet. The 5-inch differential is one reason why we find Ponderosa Pine, Colorado Spruce, Douglas Fir, and many other plants high in the hills, but not growing wild and unirrigated at the lower levels.

Increases in elevation mean decreases in temperature. The growing season at 7,000 feet is perhaps half as long as at 4,500 feet. Temperature also decreases with latitude, and a plant that has a 7,000-foot growth limit in Colorado probably has top elevation tolerance of 7,500 feet in southern New Mexico.

Sunny winter days with temperatures in the 50's cause sap to flow on the south (sunny) side of tree trunks; a precipitous drop to 20 to 25° at sundown may freeze the liquid in the cambium and result in rupture of cells and death of the bark on the southern exposure—a condition called sun scald. This is a common occurrence on thin-barked foreign imports such as maple. Natives can take it.

Early-fall and late-spring snowstorms that catch trees with leaves still on or half out are unique to the foothills country—not particularly enjoyable except to the skiing masses—and raise havoc with plants. Brittle wood imports such as Silver Maple are often badly split up. Natives have learned to shed the snow. The native evergreens are rarely damaged. Similar to this damaging phenomenon in the foothills region is the sudden, extreme temperature change, not necessarily accompanied by snow, that finds trees with sap in full flow. This weather condition has resulted in sudden death for many plants. Here again, the natives have learned to adjust.

A most practical reason for the use of natives is water conservation. The lovely lawns of Denver and other foothill cities landscaped with imported plants necessitate the use of about twice the average national consumption of water. This is in a region that has only half as much water as is available to much of the rest of the country. The use of natives could reduce our overall consumption by 25 percent. When foreign high-water demand plants are mixed with native low-water demand plants and a high-water schedule is followed, the natives tend to react by becoming grotesque in character. For example, Pinyon Pine, growing naturally to a 20-foot height and 20-foot spread might, with heavy watering, grow thin and tall to 30 feet. The excessive growth would result in a sappy and weak tree. Overwatering of large shade trees resulting in weak, fast growth exposes them to heavy snow damage and susceptibility to disease such as Dutch elm disease. For more on this aspect see section on Buffalograss, page 58.

The natives have learned to tolerate a soil condition as unique to the foothills as is the climate—alkalinity. This means that there is an excess of mineral salts in the soil. If extreme enough, nothing will grow. It is caused by two interrelated conditions: first, there is not enough precipitation to leach out the excess mineral salts, which, if removed, would render the soil more capable of supporting plant life; and second, there is not enough humus (decayed plant matter) with acidic components to create a more neutral soil better suited to plant growth. Also, the lack of humus tends to make the soil impervious and hard to cultivate. The natives tolerate alkalinity better.

The best rule of thumb is to learn the moisture and exposure conditions of the plants you want to grow and then attempt to duplicate these conditions. We emphasize the word guidelines.

Do not go into the foothills and attempt to transplant the natives. Not only is such a practice against the law, but most are very difficult to move successfully, and the odds against survival are great. Nursery stock is grown in such a way that it will withstand the shock of transplanting and then grow and prosper. Collecting wild plants is a job for experts using special equipment. They are careful to avoid damage to natural areas and usually go to considerable effort to restore collection sites to a natural condition.

Buy your natives from a reliable nursery, garden shop, or seed store. Though you may have to shop around, most of the better nurseries carry some natives while some specialize in these plants. Your nurseryperson usually will know where particular items are available and can find them for you. They may require several months' advance notice to deliver an order if, for instance, it must be dug dormant.

The third and second to last chapters cover basic landscape design concepts and planting techniques, while the last chapter explains the watering schedules referred to in the plant descriptions.

Enjoy.

Nomenclature

As our guide for both spelling and nomenclature we have used *Standardized Plant Names,* second edition, which was prepared for the American Joint Committee on Horticultural Nomenclature by Harlan P. Kelsey and William A. Payton and is considered a standard in its field. Scientific names are provided in order to avoid confusion that might arise from the many colloquial common names a single plant often has.

KEY TO TERMS

ACCENT. Plants with distinctive features such as texture, shape, or color.

BARRIER PLANT. Plants with thorns, spines, barbs, or thicket character used to control or bar access by people or animals.

GROUND COVER. Low-growing plants from 1 inch to 4 feet high generally used for covering substantial areas of ground and requiring little maintenance.

PLANT SCREEN. Plants used to block views or access from one area to another, or to control wind or noise.

SMALL GROUPED PLANTING. Arrangement of 4 to 10 plants.

LARGE GROUPED PLANTING. Arrangement of 10 to 20 plants.

MASS PLANTING. Arrangement of 20 or more plants.

SHADE TREE. A tree that attains enough height to provide a canopy for shade.

SPECIMEN. A plant that provides a feature of unique form, color, and/or texture.

DECIDUOUS TREES

Note: "Planting Space" is not specified for deciduous trees as they are not usually planted in groups.

Celtis occidentalis
COMMON HACKBERRY
(FOREIGN)

The Common Hackberry is a moderately fast-growing tree with a vaselike form. It has a light grey, corky bark and elmlike leaves. The fruit is a small, light brown berry.

The gall midge offers potential problems to the Common Hackberry. This insect attacks the buds to produce broomlike clusters of branchlets—"witches brooms." You can control the gall midge by spraying after the leaves are formed.

SUGGESTED USES—The Common Hackberry is suitable as a large, ornamental *shade or street tree.* Because it is tolerant of both dry and alkaline conditions, it is particularly valuable for our area.

HEIGHT—From *40 to 60 feet.* However, with little water, Common Hackberry may develop as a shrub, having a dwarfed and picturesque form.

WATER—Requires *schedule #2, some watering,* for a good rate of growth. Once established, this tree will withstand periods of drought, but if these conditions persist over a period of years it will become dwarfed.

EXPOSURE—Withstands full exposure to wind and grows well in either sunny or shady locations.

Crataegus succulenta
FLESHY HAWTHORN
(COLORADO) (NATIVE)

Most hawthorns develop a picturesque form and our native is no exception. It has an attractive glossy brown or yellowish stem with 1- to 1½-inch thorns and dark green, shiny leaves. In the spring, small white flowers form in clusters at the ends of twigs. These flowers produce a bright red, fleshy fruit that will attract birds in the fall.

Fleshy Hawthorn is a slow growing plant, usually only putting on 2 to 4 inches of new growth a year.

SUGGESTED USES—Fleshy Hawthorn may be used as a *tree* or *shrub* and is a good plant for *accent* use. It can be used for *accent* in tree form, and it makes an excellent *specimen plant.* Because it has spiny branches it could also be used as a *barrier.*

HEIGHT—From *10 to 20 feet* as a small tree; *up to 10 feet* as a shrub.

WATER—Requires *schedule #3, much watering,* for good growth and health.

EXPOSURE—Withstands some exposure to wind and grows best in full sun, but will grow in partially shaded locations.

SUITABLE SUBSTITUTES—Most of the locally available, cultivated varieties of hawthorns are hardy and may be used when a small, ornamental tree is desired. They all have thorns, attractive flowers, and fruit.

Elaeagnus angustifolia
RUSSIAN OLIVE
(FOREIGN)

The Russian Olive bears numerous small, fragrant, yellow flowers in the spring. These are followed by a grey or brown olivelike fruit, which is attractive to birds. The leaves are lance-shaped and silvery; the branches are also silvery and usually spiny. Russian Olive is especially tolerant of alkaline soil conditions.

SUGGESTED USES—You may use the Russian Olive as a *tree* or a *shrub* in a number of different ways: as a *specimen tree* (it develops an informal shape); as an *accent* (the silver color of its leaves provides a striking contrast to the usual foliage colors of other plants); as a *barrier* (its branches are spiny); or as a *wind screen*. This is also a very valuable tree for dry locations.

HEIGHT—From *15 to 25 feet* as a tree; from 10 to 15 feet as a shrub used in hedgerows and windscreens.

WATER—Requires *schedule #1, little watering*. Once established, the Russian Olive can withstand periods of drought, but it will become slow growing if these conditions last over a period of years.

EXPOSURE—Withstands full exposure to wind and grows well in either sun or shade.

Malus sylvestris
YELLOW TRANSPARENT APPLE
(FOREIGN)

This is the only apple tree uniquely qualified to be grown in medium to high-altitude situations. It is a tree that needs to be pruned properly to counter its normal upright growth habit. It produces a first crop in two to three years after planting. It has a tendency to bear a good crop every other year. Its main quality is earliness. It matures apples in seventy-five days after bloom.

It is considered very susceptible to fire blight disease but is resistant to cedar-apple rust. It is a good pollinator and is capable of initiating its own fruit set.

SUGGESTED USES—It can serve for *shade, shelter and screening.*

HEIGHT—From *20 to 25 feet.*

WATER Requires *schedule #2, some watering.*

EXPOSURE—Withstands normal exposure to wind. Grows best in full sun to partial sun.

SUITABLE SUBSTITUTES—Crab apples (*Malus baccata*) are generally considered good substitutes. Some of the hardier varieties have good adaptation to this region.

Populus angustifolia
NARROWLEAF POPLAR (COTTONWOOD)
(NATIVE)

The upper branches of the Narrrowleaf Poplar are white and relatively smooth. It has very narrow, willowlike leaves, which may turn a bright yellow in the fall. The cottonwoods derive their name from the masses of fuzzy cotton produced in the spring by the female trees. To avoid this, use only the male trees.

This tree sends up shoots around the trunk, which may be undesirable when a refined, highly groomed effect is desired. The branches are brittle and subject to breakage, but this is the price paid for a fast-growing tree. It is also relatively short lived, generally surviving about seventy-five years.

SUGGESTED USES—The Narrowleaf Poplar makes a good *shade tree*, particularly when a fast-growing tree is desired. It is especially valuable for high-altitude locations (up to 8,500 feet). It is more upright and narrow in its growth than most shade trees, thus lending itself to a confined location where a tree that might spreads more would be unsuitable.

HEIGHT—From *50 to 70 feet* under ideal conditions.

WATER—Requires *schedule #3, much watering*, for optimum growth.

EXPOSURE—This tree will withstand some exposure to wind and grows best in full sun, but will do well in partial shade. It is tolerant of sudden and extreme changes in the weather.

SUITABLE SUBSTITUTES—*Populus balsamifera,* Balsam Poplar (foreign), may be used in the 6,000 feet to timberline elevations. It is close in character to the Narrowleaf Poplar. This deciduous tree grows under about the same conditions as Quaking Aspen (see page 8) but is easier to transplant.

Populus sargentii
PLAINS POPLAR (COTTONWOOD)
(NATIVE)

The Plains Poplar is the common tree of the otherwise empty prairie. It is a very hardy and pest-free tree. Usually its leaves turn a clear "Aspen" yellow in the fall.

As is the case with most poplars, it is fast growing and, therefore, has brittle branches, which make it prone to breakage. All the poplar trees continually shed dead twigs, a habit that is sometimes objectionable in highly refined lawn areas. We suggest that you use only the male trees, as females produce "cotton" in the spring. The Plains Poplar produces shoots from the base of the trunk; however, these are easily pruned.

SUGGESTED USES—The Plains Poplar will grow to be massive in size. It makes a fine *shade tree* when space allows. It may develop a trunk of up to 7 feet in diameter and its branches will spread from 30 to 50 feet across.

HEIGHT—From *60 to 90 feet.*

WATER—Requires *schedule #3, much watering,* for optimum growth. It can get by with less water; however, it does not tolerate change once established.

EXPOSURE—Withstands exposure to the wind and grows best in full sun.

SUITABLE SUBSTITUTES—If you wish a smaller but similar tree, *Populus acuminata,* Lanceleaf Poplar, is a good native substitute. This tree may also be used for elevations up to 8,500 feet.

Populus tremuloides
QUAKING ASPEN
(NATIVE)

Quaking Aspen is one of the most striking of our native trees. Its many outstanding features include its white bark and "quaking" leaves. The leaves tremble or twinkle in the lightest breeze because of the flattened stem of the leaf. But, perhaps its greatest feature is its golden yellow fall color.

It reproduces mainly by suckers sent up from the roots. This aspen is relatively short lived, from 50 to 75 years. Quaking Aspen is subject to attack by cottonwood scale, which can be controlled early by spraying.

SUGGESTED USES—The Quaking Aspen is very versatile in its possible landscape uses. It can be used as an *accent,* as a *specimen,* or in *small to large grouped plantings.* It can also be used for a *small shade tree.*

HEIGHT—From *50 to 70 feet,* but on occasions may reach 80 feet.

WATER—Requires *schedule #2, some watering.* Under some conditions, such as very porous soils, schedule #3, much watering, may be required.

EXPOSURE—Withstands full exposure to wind, although this may cause a contorted, "bonsai" growth. Does best in partial shade, but will grow in full sun.

Prunus americana
AMERICAN PLUM
(NATIVE)

The bark of the American Plum is cherrylike on the branches and heavily split and peeling on older trunks, which is a very attractive characteristic. In early June, this tree has white flowers that have a particularly fine fragrance. The flowers produce a fruit that is suitable for jam or jelly.

The tree reproduces by suckers from the roots.

SUGGESTED USES—You can use the American Plum as a *tree* or as a *shrub*. Because of its attractive bark, it can be used as a *specimen tree*. It is excellent for *shade* because of its broad, flat canopy. As a shrub it can be used in *large grouped to mass plantings*. It may also be used for a *tall screen* or as a *barrier plant* as it is thicket forming and stiff with blunt twigs that resemble spines.

HEIGHT—As a tree it may occasionally reach a height of *25 to 30 feet*. Wherever it is used as a shrub, the American Plum will range from 8 to 12 feet.

WATER—Requires *schedule #2, some watering*. It will withstand moist conditions.

EXPOSURE—Withstands some exposure to wind. Grows best in partial shade, but will do well in full sun or shade.

Prunus cerasus
MONTMORENCY (SOUR) CHERRY
(FOREIGN)

The Montmorency Cherry is gene hardy in the high plains and foothills region of the Rocky Mountains. It has been known to survive extreme temperatures. It may fruit at elevations up to 8,000 feet.

It is self-pollinated and produces mature fruit in July. Once established, it has been known to succeed without irrigation.

SUGGESTED USES—It can serve as a *shade, shelter or specimen* plant.

HEIGHT—From *15 to 20 feet.*

WATER—Requires *schedule #2, some watering.*

EXPOSURE—Withstands some exposure to wind. Grows best in full to partial sun.

SUITABLE SUBSTITUTES—Dwarf varieties, Comet and Meteor (to 12 feet), and standard variety English Morello (dark sour) can also be used.

Salix amygdaloides
PEACHLEAF WILLOW
(NATIVE)

The Peachleaf Willow is our only native willow tree. It has a unique and beautiful character, which shows itself in its multistemmed trunk and picturesque form. The twigs are yellow, and the leaves turn yellow in the fall. The Peachleaf Willow is hardy and fast growing if you give it lots of water.

The branches tend to break and the tree is relatively short lived, from 50 to 75 years.

SUGGESTED USES—The picturesque shape of the Peachleaf makes it valuable as an *ornamental specimen tree*. It also may serve for *shade*.

HEIGHT—From *20 to 40 feet.*

WATER—Requires *schedule #3, much watering.*

EXPOSURE—Withstands some exposure to wind and grows best in partial shade, although it will grow in full sun or shade.

SUITABLE SUBSTITUTES—The *Salix babylonica* 'Golden', Golden Weeping Willow, is a similar, foreign, very hardy tree. It attains a height of 20 to 40 feet and also has yellow twigs.

EVERGREEN TREES

Note: "Planting Space" is not specified
for evergreen trees as they are not
usually planted in groups.

Juniperus monosperma
ONE-SEED JUNIPER
(NATIVE)

The One-seed Juniper is a small, multistemmed, block-shaped evergreen. It has small, scalelike needles, which range from yellow-green to blue-green in color. The berrylike fruit is usually reddish yellow-brown or bluish in color and is tasty to birds and other wildlife. If you have alkaline soil this tree will be of special interest to you as it is tolerant of alkaline conditions. Unlike the Rocky Mountain Juniper (see page 15), which tends to become brownish or purplish in the winter, the One-seed Juniper retains a true green color.

SUGGESTED USES—This makes an excellent *specimen tree,* because it can be very picturesque. It can serve as a high evergreen *screen* and under difficult conditions, it is suitable for use as a clipped hedge.

HEIGHT—Generally from *15 to 20 feet;* but under optimum conditions, may reach as high as 50 feet.

WATER—Requires *schedule #1, little watering*. Very drought resistant.

EXPOSURE—Withstands full exposure to wind and grows best in full sun, but will withstand some shade.

Juniperus scopulorum
ROCKY MOUNTAIN JUNIPER
(NATIVE)

The Rocky Mountain Juniper is a slow-growing tree whose form varies from a dense, one-stemmed, symmetrical pyramid to a dwarfed, open, irregular, multistemmed shape. The needles are scalelike and vary in color from brownish-green to green to silver-blue. Your nurseryperson should be able to help you decide which tree will fit your particular needs and wants.

The fruit is blue and berrylike. Although these berries were once part of the diet of Native Americans, they are not delicious.

SUGGESTED USES—This is a versatile tree, having several landscape uses. If space allows, it is very effective in *small grouped plantings.* Because it is an evergreen it can be used for *accent.* It also makes an excellent *screen* against objectionable views or wind. In its multistemmed form it is fine as a *specimen plant.*

HEIGHT—Generally from *15 to 20 feet,* but occasionally grows to 50 feet.

WATER—Requires *schedule #1, little watering.* Very drought resistant. Watering during long dry spells in the winter is a good idea.

EXPOSURE—Withstands full exposure to wind and grows well in either sunny or shady locations.

SUITABLE SUBSTITUTES—Most of the locally available, cultivated upright junipers are hardy and may be used in place of both the One-seed Juniper and the Rocky Mountain Juniper. However, the cultivated varieties are all generally well formed and symmetrical and are not as picturesque and natural as the native varieties.

Picea pungens
COLORADO BLUE SPRUCE
(NATIVE)

The Colorado Spruce is probably our best known and most often used native evergreen. In its bluest shades, it has a kind of beauty not found in any other tree. It varies in color, though, from green to blue-green to silvery blue. The last color is most striking, and, therefore, most desired and most expensive. The needles are stiff and prickly.

The spruce gall aphid and the tussock moth may attack this tree. If you don't destroy these pests by spraying, the tree may die.

SUGGESTED USES—The Colorado Spruce has a wide variety of uses—as a *specimen, accent, or shade tree.* You might even try it in a clipped, formal hedge.

HEIGHT—Generally from *60 to 70 feet,* but may reach a height of up to 120 feet.

WATER—Requires *schedule #3, much watering,* for best growth, but can get by with schedule #2, some watering, once the tree is established. An occasional soaking during the winter will help summer growth.

EXPOSURE—Withstands some exposure to wind. It does well in either full sun or shade.

Pinus aristata
BRISTLECONE (FOXTAIL) PINE
(NATIVE)

The Bristlecone Pine has short, tiff needles that surround the twigs like a bottle brush, giving it a "foxtail" appearance. This characteristic sets it apart from the other pines and gives it its colloquial name. It has an irregular growth habit and becomes very picturesque with age. It is very slow growing, however, putting on only 2 to 4 inches a year. If you wish to plant a tree for future generations to enjoy this would be a good choice, as ring dating has shown that some specimens of the Bristlecone Pine are the oldest known living things on Earth.

SUGGESTED USES—The "foxtail" appearance of the Bristlecone makes it an excellent *specimen plant.* It may also be used for *shade.*

HEIGHT—Generally from *30 to 40 feet,* but under ideal conditions can grow to 60 feet.

WATER—Will do best with *schedule #2, some watering*, but once established, it can withstand dry conditions.

EXPOSURE—Enjoys a windy exposure and grows best in full sun.

Pinus cembroides edulis
COLORADO PINYON PINE
(NATIVE)

The best attribute of the Colorado Pinyon Pine is its size; it's the only small- to medium-size native pine, and this makes it useful in situations where other evergreen trees may be too large. This is a hardy and relatively slow-growing tree, extending 2 to 6 inches a year.

The cones produce large seeds, which are edible and taste good. They are often collected for food and are available at many stores. At one time, Indians native to the region ate the inner bark of the Pinyon during periods of famine.

SUGGESTED USES—The Colorado Pinyon Pine is an excellent plant for a *high, evergreen screen.* It can also be used for *accent* or as a *specimen plant.* Practically all Pinyon trees sold have been collected from the wild and are relatively inexpensive and easy to transplant.

HEIGHT—Generally from *10 to 15 feet,* but under ideal conditions can grow to 40 feet.

WATER—Requires *schedule #1, little water.* The Colorado Pinyon Pine withstands drought very well; in fact, it prefers well-drained, dry situations.

EXPOSURE—Withstands full exposure to wind and grows best in full sun.

Pinus ponderosa
PONDEROSA PINE
(NATIVE)

The Ponderosa Pine is large and massive. A unique characteristic is the dark orange color of the bark on older trees. Because it is drought resistant, heat tolerant, and very hardy, it is one of the most important of our native ornamental evergreens.

The bark beetle and mistletoe attack this tree. The bark beetle bores tunnels under the bark and can kill a weak tree. Mistletoe is a parasitic plant that also can kill a tree. Our native mistletoe is not as attractive as that used for Christmas, having yellow-green, scalelike leaves.

SUGGESTED USES—The Ponderosa Pine is well suited for use as a *specimen, accent, or shade tree*. When young it is well formed; as it matures it becomes irregular.

HEIGHT—From *60 to 80 feet;* some individuals may reach as high as 150 feet.

WATER—Requires *schedule #1, little watering*, and prefers a dry situation. It can tolerate moisture, but if grown in moist conditions it requires good drainage.

EXPOSURE—Withstands full exposure to wind and grows best in a sunny location, but will grow in partial shade.

Pseudotsuga taxifolia
DOUGLAS FIR
(NATIVE)

The Douglas Fir is very similar to the Colorado Blue Spruce in its color range (green to blue-green) and form. There are differences in the needle, though. If the needles are stiff and prickly, it's a spruce; if they're soft, it's a Douglas Fir.

Douglas Fir retains its lower branches well and is drought resistant.

It is an alternate host of the spruce gall aphid and should not be planted next to spruce. The tussock moth attacks this tree and will kill it slowly, beginning at the tip of the leader, if a protective spray is not used.

SUGGESTED USES—The Douglas Fir is one of our native evergreen trees that does not get as much landscape use as it might. It can be used for *accent* and as a *specimen.* You may also use it effectively to create a *large screen planting.* It is especially valuable for shady locations or northern exposures.

HEIGHT—Generally from *60 to 70 feet;* but may reach as high as 130 feet.

WATER—Requires *schedule #2, some watering.* Once established this tree will withstand considerable drought.

EXPOSURE—Withstands some exposure to wind. Grows best in partial shade or a northern exposure, but will grow in full sun or shade.

SUITABLE SUBSTITUTE—Also similar in characteristics is the native *Abies concolor,* White Fir. White Fir also has many of the characteristics of Colorado Spruce, tending to be almost as blue as the bluer types of Colorado Spruce.

DECIDUOUS SHRUBS

Acer glabrum
Rocky Mountain Maple
(native)

The most distinguishing feature of the Rocky Mountain Maple is its deep, three-lobed leaf. In the fall, these leaves turn pale yellow and the tree sheds its leaves that are close to the ground. The seed is of the typical "winged" variety and is very attractive, ranging in color from green to yellow to red.

SUGGESTED USES—The Rocky Mountain Maple can be very graceful and is best used as a single *specimen plant.* It might also be used as a single small tree or in *small grouped plantings.*

PLANTING SPACE—From *5 to 8 feet.*

HEIGHT—From *10 to 25 feet.*

WATER—Requires *schedule #2, some watering,* for best growth, but will withstand limited drought conditions of two to three months.

EXPOSURE—The Rocky Mountain Maple tolerates some exposure to wind and does best in partial shade, although it will grow in full sun or shade.

SUITABLE SUBSTITUTES—Two of the cultivated maples, *Acer ginnala,* Amur Maple, and *Acer tataricum,* Tatarian Maple, are similar in character to the Rocky Mountain Maple though *Acer tataricum* tends to be more treelike in form.

Amorpha fruticosa
INDIGOBUSH AMORPHA
(NATIVE)

In late June or early July the Indigobush Amorpha is covered with spikes of pealike, indigo flowers. These flowers produce small seed pods, which often remain on the plant throughout the winter. The leaves are comprised of nine to twenty-five very small leaflets. This shrub is especially tolerant of alkaline soils.

SUGGESTED USES—Indigo Amorpha tends to be "leggy," or loose-stemmed and is best used in *large grouped or mass plantings,* which will give more body to the plant.

PLANTING SPACE—From *4 to 6 feet.*

HEIGHT—Generally from *6 to 10 feet,* but can grow to 15 feet.

WATER—Requires *schedule #3, much watering,* for best growth, but will do well on schedule #2, some watering, and will even withstand drought.

EXPOSURE—Withstands some exposure to wind and grows best in full sun.

SUITABLE SUBSTITUTE—*Amorpha canescens,* Lead Plant Amorpha (foreign), is similar to the Indigobush Amorpha, but grows only 1 to 2 feet high. It may be used where a smaller shrub is needed.

Artemisia sp.
SAGEBRUSH
(NATIVE)

Most of the sagebrush commercially available have silver-gray foliage and are distinctively aromatic.

SUGGESTED USES—You will find there is a varied selection of sagebrush. They all best lend themselves to landscape use in *small grouped plantings,* or may be used for *accent.*

PLANTING SPACE—Varies depending on height of the particular type but the general rule is from half to three-quarters of the height of mature plant. Your nurseryperson will be able to help you with this.

HEIGHT—Those available for landscape use range from *1 to 4 feet.*

WATER—Requires *schedule #1, little watering.* Sagebrush is very drought resistant.

EXPOSURE—Withstands full exposure to wind and grows best in full sun; will do well in partial shade.

Cercocarpus montanus
TRUE MOUNTAIN MAHOGANY
(NATIVE)

True Mountain Mahogany produces a unique spiral seed plume. These mature in the fall and remain throughout the winter, giving the shrub an attractive silvery appearance, especially when the sun shines on them. Some seasons the leaves may have good yellow to red fall color. This is a very hardy shrub, which can be made more compact in growth by pruning.

SUGGESTED USES—The True Mountain Mahogany is best used in *small grouped to mass plantings*. It can also be grown as a single *specimen* as its unusual seeds make it a very interesting plant.

PLANTING SPACE—From *4 to 6 feet*.

HEIGHT—Generally from *4 to 8 feet*, but may grow as high as 20 feet.

WATER—Requires *schedule #1, little watering.* This shrub is very drought resistant.

EXPOSURE—Withstands full exposure to wind. It grows best in full sun, but will do well in partial shade.

Cornus stolonifera coloradadensis
COLORADO REDOSIER (REDTWIG) DOGWOOD
(NATIVE)

Colorado Redosier (Redtwig) Dogwood is a hardy, well-formed shrub that has a bright red stem and white berries. Birds are attracted to the berries in winter. The white flower clusters are inconspicuous. This shrub has a uniform growth habit.

SUGGESTED USES—Colorado Redosier, or Redtwig Dogwood, is one of our most striking native shrubs, particularly as a winter *accent* when its bright red twigs provide a colorful contrast to the white snow. In summer the twigs are concealed and not at all noticeable. This plant is also suitable as a *screen.*

PLANTING SPACE—Every *4 feet.*

HEIGHT—From *4 to 6 feet.*

WATER—Requires *schedule #3, much watering*.

EXPOSURE—Withstands some exposure to wind and grows well in either full sun or partial shade.

SUITABLE SUBSTITUTE—*Cornus stolonifera flaviramea,* Yellow-stem Dogwood (foreign), is similar in character to the Colorado Redosier Dogwood except that instead of a bright red stem it has a bright golden-yellow stem; again this makes it particularly valuable for winter accent, especially in combination with evergreens. It is not as hardy as the Redosier.

Physocarpos monogynus
MOUNTAIN NINEBARK
(NATIVE)

In May the Mountain Ninebark has small clusters of white flowers resembling those of the Bridal Wreath Spirea. The flowers last for about five days and produce an attractive reddish-brown seed head. Bark on the older stems is continuously shredding off in strips, leaving several shades of brown. This process accounts for the name ninebark (nine colors of bark).

Ninebark produces suckers from the roots.

SUGGESTED USES—If you want to plant an area that is in full shade, the Mountain Ninebark is one of the best shrubs you can use. It is best used in *small to large grouped plantings.*

PLANTING SPACE—From *3 to 4 feet.*

HEIGHT—Low and spreading; attains a height of *3 to 4 feet.*

WATER—Requires *schedule #2, some watering.*

EXPOSURE—Withstands some exposure to wind. It grows best in shady locations.

SUITABLE SUBSTITUTES—Many of the other locally available varieties are also hardy. They range from 3 to 8 feet in height and are similar in character to the Mountain Ninebark.

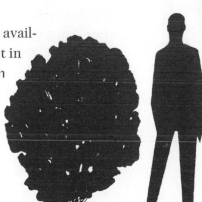

Potentilla fruticosa
BUSH CINQUEFOIL
(NATIVE)

One of the great attributes of this plant is the yellow, roselike flowers, which bloom continuously from early summer to fall. Bush Cinquefoil is a well-formed shrub, requiring little or no pruning.

SUGGESTED USES—Bush Cinquefoil and its cultivated varieties are some of our most valuable landscaping shrubs. They are versatile and may be used as *specimen plants,* in *small to large grouped plantings,* for *accent,* and even as a *tall ground cover.*

PLANTING SPACE—From *3 to 4 feet.*

HEIGHT—From *3 to 4 feet.*

WATER—Requires *schedule #2, some watering,* but will do well in dry or wet conditions.

EXPOSURE—Withstands full exposure to wind. It grows well in either full sun or shade.

SUITABLE SUBSTITUTES—Most of the locally available varieties are similar to Bush Cinquefoil with only minor differences. Most average 3 to 4 feet in height. A notable exception is the horticultural type known as "Sutter's Gold," which has low-arching branches and grows only 2 feet high. This variety makes an excellent ground cover.

Prunus besseyi
WESTERN SAND CHERRY
(NATIVE)

Particularly appreciated for its superb hardiness, the Western Sand Cherry can be a very fine small shrub. It has small white flowers and produces a small fruit that is both edible and attractive to native birds.

SUGGESTED USES—Plant as a *barrier* along fence rows or windbreaks, also over gentle to steep slopes.

PLANTING SPACE— From *18 to 30 inches*.

HEIGHT— From *2 to 3 feet*.

WATER—Requires *schedule #3, much watering*.

EXPOSURE—Very hardy in almost any situation or exposure.

SUITABLE SUBSTITUTES—Several plum cherry hybrids like *Prunus opata* are considered productive and hardy.

Prunus virginiana demissa
WESTERN CHOKECHERRY
(NATIVE)

The Western Chokecherry can be an attractive large shrub. It has clusters of small, white flowers in May or June. The fruit is black when ripe and is too tart to eat raw, but makes very good jelly, jam, or syrup. If you want to use the fruit for one of these purposes you'll have to keep an eye on it, because it's also very popular with wildlife, particularly birds.

SUGGESTED USES—The Western Chokecherry can be used in *small grouped to mass plantings;* it can also be used for a *tall, screen planting.*

PLANTING SPACE—From *6 to 8 feet.*

HEIGHT—Generally from *10 to 15 feet,* but may reach as high as 25 feet.

WATER—Requires *schedule #2, some watering.* Does well in conditions ranging from moist to dry and is drought resistant.

EXPOSURE—Withstands some exposure to wind. It will grow in sunny or partly shady locations.

Quercus gambelii
GAMBEL (SCRUB) OAK
(NATIVE)

Like all oaks, the Gambel Oak produces acorns. This shrub has a rounded lobe, typical white-oak leaf, which occasionally has good brown to orange fall color.

It produces root suckers and is slow growing, generally putting on only a couple of inches a year.

SUGGESTED USES—The Gambel Oak is another plant that is suitable for use as either a *tree or shrub*. As a tree it develops a rather loose, picturesque form and makes an excellent *specimen*. It can also be used as a small *shade tree*. As a shrub it lends itself naturally to *small to large grouped plantings*. It may also be used as a *plant screen*.

PLANTING SPACE—From *2 to 5 feet*, depending on density of screen.

HEIGHT—Generally *5 to 15 feet*, but may grow to 35 feet.

WATER—Requires *schedule #2, some watering*, but can withstand dry conditions.

EXPOSURE—Withstands full exposure to wind. Grows in either sunny or partly shady locations.

Rhus glabra cismontana
ROCKY MOUNTAIN SMOOTH SUMAC
(NATIVE)

The Rocky Mountain Smooth Sumac is similar to the cultivated Smooth Sumac, but is lower growing and more shrublike. Its leaves have nine to seventeen leaflets, which turn brilliant red in the fall. It produces red berries attractive to birds. Smooth Sumac root suckers freely.

Native Americans in the region used this plant for many purposes—the roots for dye, the leaves and bark for tannic acid, the berries for food, and various outer parts for medicine. The red berries are acidic and can be used to make a lemonadelike drink.

SUGGESTED USES—If you want to cover a steep bank in a dry location with something other than grass, Rocky Mountain Smooth Sumac is an excellent choice. It is particularly suited for use as a *tall ground cover,* as well as for *small grouped to mass plantings* and *accent plantings*.

PLANTING SPACE—From *3 to 4 feet*.

HEIGHT—From *2 to 5 feet*.

WATER—Requires *schedule #1, little watering,* but will grow in moist locations if it has good drainage.

EXPOSURE—Withstands some exposure to wind. Grows best in full sun, but will grow in partial shade.

Rhus trilobata
THREE-LEAF (SKUNKBUSH) SUMAC
(NATIVE)

The Three-leaf Sumac is a generally well-shaped, compact shrub. The flowers are yellow, grow in rather inconspicuous clusters and produce clusters of red berries. The berries produce a sticky substance which may collect cobwebs and dust, creating an untidy appearance. If this occurs the shrubs can be "washed" with occasional sprinklings.

Like the berries of Smooth Sumac the berries of Three-leaf Sumac produce an acidic taste, and a handful stirred in water with sugar will afford a surprisingly good-tasting substitute for lemonade. Hikers find that a few berries placed in the mouth and sucked on will produce a refreshing, lemony taste.

The Native Americans also had many uses for this shrub. They ate the berries and used the stems for weaving baskets. The berries are also attractive to birds.

SUGGESTED USES—The Three-leaf Sumac is best used in *small grouped to mass plantings.* It may also be used for a *tall ground cover* in difficult situations and is particularly valuable for use in dry locations. The shrub produces a disagreeable odor when crushed, hence the name "Skunkbush."

PLANTING SPACE—From *3 to 4 feet.*

HEIGHT—Generally from *3 to 5 feet,* but may grow to 8 feet.

WATER—Requires *schedule #1, little watering.* It is very drought resistant.

EXPOSURE—Withstands full exposure to wind. Grows best in full sun, but will grow in partial shade.

Ribes aureum
GOLDEN CURRANT
(NATIVE)

   The Golden Currant has a fragrant, tube-shaped, yellow flower, which produces a yellow or black berry. You can use these berries to make a very flavorful jam. The berries also attract birds.

   This is another plant that roots suckers.

SUGGESTED USES—Golden Currant is another shrub you will find particularly valuable for dry locations. It is best used in *small grouped to mass plantings*. It can also be used for a *medium-height plant screen*.

PLANTING SPACE—From *3 to 3½ feet*.

HEIGHT—Generally from *3 to 4 feet*, but may reach 6 feet.

WATER—Requires *schedule #1, little watering*, and is tolerant of drought or moist conditions.

EXPOSURE—Withstands some exposure to wind and grows best in full sun.

Ribes inerme
WHITESTEM GOOSEBERRY
(NATIVE)

The Whitestem Gooseberry has long, gracefully arching stems that are heavily armed with sharp spines. Its flowers are in clusters of two to four and are greenish or pink in color. They produce a tart, black fruit, which is excellent for jam or syrup ... if you can collect them before the birds do.

SUGGESTED USES—The Whitestem Gooseberry is best used in *small grouped plantings* or used as a *screen*. If you ever walk into one you will discover that it is also excellent for *barrier plantings*.

PLANTING SPACE—From *4 to 6 feet*.

HEIGHT—From *3 to 5 feet*.

WATER—Requires *schedule #3, much watering,* for best growth, but once established could get by on schedule #2, some watering.

EXPOSURE—Will not withstand much exposure to wind. Grows in either full sun or partial shade.

SUITABLE SUBSTITUTES—*Ribes grossularia hirtellum* and varieties Colossal and Pixwell are extremely hardy hybrids desirable for their fruiting characteristics.

Rosa sp.
WILD ROSE
(NATIVE)

The Wild Rose has fragrant, pink to white flowers that bloom in June and produce red fruit (hip). The hip may remain into the winter, thus providing additional color. Hips are tasty to both birds and people. They make a fine jelly and are very rich in vitamins. Both the flower petals and the fruit were used by Native Americans for medicinal purposes.

Wild Rose root suckers extensively.

SUGGESTED USES—The Wild Rose will be most attractive when used in *small grouped to large grouped plantings.* Because the stems are spiny it may also serve as a *low barrier planting.*

PLANTING SPACE—From *18 inches to 2 feet.*

HEIGHT—From *2 to 4 feet.*

WATER—Requires *schedule #1, little watering,* but will grow under moist conditions if well drained.

EXPOSURE—Withstands some exposure to wind; grows well in either full sun or shade.

Rubus deliciosus
THIMBLEBERRY (BOULDER RASPBERRY)
(NATIVE)

The Thimbleberry has large, beautiful, white rose-like flowers in late May. Its branches are graceful, arching, and spineless. The flowers produce a raspberrylike fruit that is more seed than flesh unless the plant has been well watered. The fruit can be either very tasty or very tart and is a favorite food of birds.

SUGGESTED USES—Thimbleberry is one of our most attractive native shrubs, and as such it makes an excellent *specimen plant*. You may also use it in *small grouped plantings*, as a *medium-high hedge* or *screen*, and for *accent*.

PLANTING SPACE—From *3 to 5 feet*.

HEIGHT—From *3 to 5 feet*.

WATER—Requires *schedule #2, some watering*, but will withstand dry conditions.

EXPOSURE—Withstands little exposure to wind. Will grow in either full sun or shade, but does best in partial shade.

SUITABLE SUBSTITUTES—*Rubus strigosus*, American Red Raspberry (native), is another shrub that you might use. Its flowers are small and fragrant; its branches are very spiny; and its fruit is very tasty. The fruit can be used for jam or jelly and it too is favored by birds.

EVERGREEN AND
BROADLEAF EVERGREEN SHRUBS

Cercocarpus ledifolius
Curl-leaf Mountain Mahogany
(Native)

   Curl-leaf Mountain Mahogany retains its leaves for two years, thus making it one of the few broadleaf evergreens native to the Rocky Mountains (Utah). It has a good form. The flowers and spiral-tailed seed are similar to the deciduous True Mountain Mahogany (see page 25). It is somewhat slow growing, putting on only 4 to 6 inches of new growth a year.

SUGGESTED USES—The Curl-leaf Mountain Mahogany is probably the hardiest broadleaf evergreen shrub we have available. It is particularly valuable as a *specimen plant*. It works well as *small grouped plantings* or as a tall, evergreen *plant screen*.

PLANTING SPACE—From *4 to 6 feet*.

HEIGHT—Generally *5 to 15 feet*, but may reach as high as 30 feet.

WATER—Requires *schedule #1, little watering*.

EXPOSURE—Withstands some exposure to wind and grows best in full sun.

Juniperas communis saxatilis
MOUNTAIN COMMON JUNIPER
(NATIVE)

Mountain Common Juniper comes in a variety of bright greens. Its color sets it apart from the other spreading junipers and is its greatest value. The fruit is a bluish berry that remains on the plant for several years. This plant varies in form, but is generally low and spreading.

SUGGESTED USES—The Mountain Common Juniper is a native spreading juniper that can be planted as an *accent, ground cover, or specimen.*

PLANTING SPACE—From *4 to 6 feet.*

HEIGHT—From *1 to 3 feet* and often spreads as much as 10 feet.

WATER—Requires *schedule #2, some watering,* but will withstand dry conditions.

EXPOSURE—Withstands some exposure to wind. Grows best in partial shade, although it will grow in full sun. It may winter burn (i.e., develop brown patches).

SUITABLE SUBSTITUTES—Most of the locally available spreading junipers are hardy and may be used in our area. They come in a variety of colors (green, blue-green, golden, gray-green, and silver) and a variety of forms (creeping, low spreading, and regular spreading).

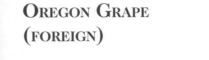

Mahonia aquifolium
OREGON GRAPE
(FOREIGN)

The most familiar feature of the Oregon Grape is its shiny, hollylike leaves that become purple-red during the winter. This very useful broadleaf has bright yellow flowers, which produce a blue-black berry good for jelly. The berries are also a favorite food of birds.

SUGGESTED USES—The Oregon Grape is a striking broadleaf evergreen. It is best suited for use as a *specimen or accent*. It may be used to create a hedge and can be shaped by pruning. It should only be used in a protected location.

PLANTING SPACE—From *4 to 6 feet.*

HEIGHT— From *4 to 6 feet.*

WATER—Requires *schedule #3, much watering.*

EXPOSURE—Will not withstand much exposure to wind and does best in partial shade—do not plant in a location with a southern exposure. It is very vulnerable to winter burn.

SUITABLE SUBSTITUTES—*Mahonia aquifolium compacta,* Compact Oregon Grape (foreign), has the same characteristics as the Oregon Grape, but its ultimate height is only 4 feet. It may be used when a smaller shrub is desired.

Pinus mugo mughus
MUGHO SWISS MOUNTAIN PINE
(FOREIGN)

The Mugho Swiss Mountain Pine is an especially attractive evergreen shrub. It has the characteristics and color of pine trees.

SUGGESTED USES—This is another spreading type of evergreen and offers an excellent alternative to spreading junipers. You may use it as an *accent or specimen*. It can also be planted in *small to large grouped plantings* or for a *high plant screen*.

PLANTING SPACE—From *5 to 10 feet* is recommended, depending upon how it is used. If you plan to keep it low, then the minimum planting space should be used.

HEIGHT—Can be kept low, *2 to 4 feet,* by pruning the candles (new growth) each spring; if kept low it can spread as much as 10 feet across.

WATER—Requires *schedule #2, some water.* Once established, Mugho Swiss Mountain Pine can tolerate dry conditions.

EXPOSURE—Withstands some exposure to wind. Grows well in either full sun or partial shade.

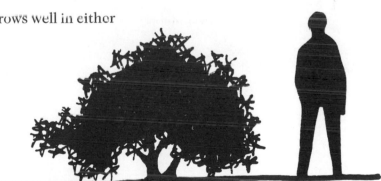

GROUND COVERS

Arctostaphylos uva-ursi
KINNIKINNICK (BEARBERRY)
(NATIVE)

Kinnikinnick is a broadleaf evergreen vine with small, leathery leaves. It has small, fragrant, white or pink, bell-shaped, waxy flowers that produce a green berrylike fruit that turns red over winter

The Kinnikinnick is an interesting plant, having been used by both the Native Americans and early settlers for a number of purposes. Native Americans used it as a medicine, tea, and tobacco and for curing skins. The settlers added to its uses by making cider and jelly with its berries. The berries are also a favorite of birds and other wildlife.

This plant may take a little extra effort in soil preparation. It likes a well-drained, sandy, slightly acidic soil, but it is worth the trouble.

SUGGESTED USES—Kinnikinnick can be used simply as a *ground cover* or *accent*.

PLANTING SPACE—From *1 to 3 feet,* depending on how quickly you want a full effect. It is relatively slow growing, spreading 2 to 4 inches a year.

HEIGHT—Forms a mat of *3 to 6 inches.*

WATER—Requires *schedule #2, some watering*, for best growth. If it is well drained, it will withstand moist conditions. Once it has been established it will also grow in dry locations.

EXPOSURE—Withstands some exposure to wind. It grows best in partial or full shade. It will do well in full sun, although it may need some protection until established.

Antennaria sp.
PUSSYTOES
(NATIVE)

Pussytoes is an evergreen closely related to the edelweiss of Europe with very attractive silver-gray leaves clothed in soft, short hairs. The small white to pink flowers are not prominent. We think you will find this a delightful plant to use.

SUGGESTED USES—Pussytoes is a *ground cover* that may be used as such, or, because of its unique silver-gray leaves, it may also be used for *accent*.

PLANTING SPACE—This plant can be bought in 3-inch pots or in sodlike strips. The plants bought in pots should be planted about *1 foot apart*. If bought as sod, break the strips into 3-inch pieces and plant the pieces about 1 foot apart. Pussytoes will spread and fill in the open space in about two years.

HEIGHT—Forms a mat of *1 to 3 inches*.

WATER—Requires *schedule #2, some watering*. However, it can withstand dry conditions and is particularly valuable for this reason.

EXPOSURE—Withstands some exposure to wind. It will grow in conditions ranging from full sun to shade, but does best in partial shade or full shade. It may need some protection while getting established if planted in full sun.

Clematis sp.
CLEMATIS
(NATIVE)

The Clematis vine has star-shaped white, yellow, or lavender flowers and produces an attractive, fuzzy seed head that remains on the plant all winter. Your nurseryperson can advise which plants will have the color of flower you desire.

SUGGESTED USES—You may use Clematis in *small grouped to mass plantings;* as *ground cover,* particularly on steep slopes where other plants may not grow well; or you may use them individually as trailing vines on fences, and so on.

PLANTING SPACE—From *2 to 4 feet.*

HEIGHT—These vines will grow to be *5 to 20 feet in length.*

WATER—Requires sched*ule #2, some watering,* but once established can tolerate dry conditions.

EXPOSURE—Withstands some exposure to wind and will grow in full sun or partial shade.

Echinocactus sp., Mamillaria sp., and Opuntia sp.
BARREL, PINCUSHION, AND PRICKLY PEAR CACTI
(NATIVES)

These cacti have very attractive flowers ranging in color from pink to yellow, orange, lavender, purple, and rose. All of these have fleshy, evergreen-colored, spiny-covered parts throughout. Some species of the Prickly Pear have a very tasty, edible fruit.

SUGGESTED USES—Cacti can be used individually as *accent* or *specimen* plants, or as *grouped plants*. You may also use them as a *low barrier planting*.

PLANTING SPACE—From *a few inches to 2 feet*. Your nurseryperson will be able to tell you exactly how to space any particular cactus.

HEIGHT—These cacti range from *a few inches to about 1 foot*.

WATER—Requires *schedule #1, little watering*.

EXPOSURE—Withstands full exposure to wind. Needs a location with full sun.

Fragaria sp.
WILD STRAWBERRY
(NATIVE)

The Wild Strawberry has a small white flower that produces small $\frac{1}{4}$-inch berries. While these berries are small, they are a real delicacy and well worth your extra effort. You will have to fight the birds for them, though. Like all strawberries they reproduce by runners.

SUGGESTED USES—Wild Strawberry is doubly useful as a *ground cover* and a food source.

PLANTING SPACE—Every *12 inches.*

HEIGHT—From *1 to 4 inches.*

WATER—Requires *schedule #2, some watering.* It will grow in moist locations and will tolerate some drought, but it will not fruit well under drought conditions.

EXPOSURE—Withstands little exposure to wind. It grows well in either full sun or shade.

SUITABLE SUBSTITUTES—There are a variety of hardy, cultivated strawberries that are available and may be used instead of the Wild Strawberry, especially if the larger fruit is preferred.

Mahonia repens
CREEPING MAHONIA
(NATIVE)

Like the Oregon Grape (see page 42), the Creeping Mahonia has hollylike, evergreen leaves, which turn slightly red or purple during winter. The clusters of small yellow flowers produce blue-black berries that can be used to make jelly.

SUGGESTED USES—In addition to providing *ground cover,* Creeping Mahonia also gives *accent.*

PLANTING SPACE—Every *12 inches.*

HEIGHT—Up to *12 inches.*

WATER—Requires *schedule #2, some watering.* It is drought resistant.

EXPOSURE—Withstands some exposure to wind, but does best in protected locations. It grows best in partial shade, but will grow in either full sun or shade.

Stachys lantana
LAMB'S EAR
(NATIVE)

Attractive at all times of the year, gray-leaved Lamb's Ear or Lamb's Tongue forms a closely packed mat impenetrable by most weeds. It is named for its soft lime-white woolly leaves. During summer it produces spikes of small purplish flowers about 12 inches high. With a small increase over natural watering, the plant will spread rapidly over a large area. It can be increased by collecting and spreading its seed or by tearing off rooted offsets and transporting them to new areas where they are to grow.

SUGGESTED USES—*Ground cover* and *edging*.

PLANTING SPACE—*12 to 18 inches*.

HEIGHT—up to *6 inches*.

WATER SCHEDULE—Requires *schedule #2, some watering*. It is drought resistant.

EXPOSURE—Sun or partial shade.

Yucca glauca
SMALL SOAPWEED (SPANISH BAYONET)
(NATIVE)

The Small Soapweed has long, stiff, pointed ever-green leaves. These leaves are usually less than 1/2-inch wide. The bell-shaped flowers are a striking creamy white, and are carried on 2- to 3-foot stalks that rise from the center of clumps.

Native Americans used this plant in a variety of ways. The leaves were used to make ropes, baskets, brushes, mats, blankets, and soaps. The buds, flowers, seeds, and stalks were used for food and medicine. Total use!

SUGGESTED USES—In a *small grouped to mass planting* as *ground cover,* for a *low barrier planting,* as a *specimen,* or for *accent.*

PLANTING SPACE—Every *2 feet.*

HEIGHT—From *1 to 2 1/2 feet.*

WATER—Requires *schedule #1, little watering.* This plant will toler-ate severe drought.

EXPOSURE—Withstands full exposure to wind. Grows best in full sun, but will grow in partial shade.

SUITABLE SUBSTITUTES—Most of the locally available yucca are simi-lar in character and may be substituted. Of particular note is *Yucca baccata,* Indian Banana (native), which has wider 1 1/2 inch leaves. This yucca has curled fibers along the edges, and is very ornamental. How-ever, north of southern Colorado, it is not hardy and should be used in somewhat protected locations.

GRASSES

Arundo donax
GIANT REED
(FOREIGN)

The Giant Reed has brownish-white flower panicles (a loose, compound flower cluster) and bamboolike stems.

SUGGESTED USES—This is a strikingly ornamental grass that can be used individually or in *small grouped plantings* as an *accent* or *specimen.*

PLANTING SPACE—Every *3 to 5 feet.*

HEIGHT—Up to *12 feet.*

WATER—Requires *schedule #3, much watering.*

EXPOSURE—Withstands some exposure to wind, but does best in protected locations. Grows best in full sun, but will grow in partial shade.

SUITABLE SUBSTITUTES—*Arundo donax versicolor,* Whitestripe Giant Reed, may also be used. It is similar to the Giant Reed, except it has green- and white-striped leaves and is not quite as hardy.

Avena sterilis
BLUE AVENA (ANIMATED OAT GRASS)
(FOREIGN)

The Blue Avena is a graceful clump grass with a bluish cast to its leaves. It has white spikes (flowers or seeds arranged on a common elongated axis). When dried, the long awns (tail-like bristles) of the seeds twist and turn with the variance of moisture in the air, hence the name "Animated Oat Grass."

SUGGESTED USES—Blue Avena is not suited for lawn use. You may use it individually or in *small grouped plantings* as an *accent* or *specimen*. It could possibly be used in *mass planting as a tall ground cover*, but this would require considerable maintenance.

PLANTING SPACE—Every *3 to 4 feet*.

HEIGHT—From *2 to 3 feet*.

WATER—Requires *schedule #2, some watering*.

EXPOSURE—Withstands some exposure to wind. Grows best in full sun, but will grow in partial shade.

Buchloe dactyloides
BUFFALOGRASS
(NATIVE)

Buffalograss is particularly suited for use in the Rocky Mountains. Because it is a native prairie grass it needs little water, about 15 inches annually as compared to about 36 inches for Bluegrass. At its native height it is about 4 inches tall. It requires less mowing, perhaps only three to four times a summer, or perhaps no mowing if used in a totally natural area. Of our native grasses it is the only one that takes much wear and tear. However, for areas that receive a large amount of wear (athletic fields, etc.) Bluegrass is preferred.

SUGGESTED USES—Buffalograss should be considered as a design option rather than an across-the-board substitute for Bluegrass. For instance, Bluegrass is generally preferred for the front lawn because of its better color and more refined look. On the other hand, Buffalograss for the rear lawn and/or remote corners of your property is preferred. Also, Buffalograss is the perfect filler for small areas such as hot spots along south-facing curbs and walls where Bluegrass will not thrive or places not reached by your sprinkler.

Being a warm-season grass, Buffalograss is green only during the warm season months (May through September), and even then it does not have the intense, emerald green of Bluegrass. Rather it is slightly silvery in color. These negative aspects, when compared to Bluegrass, can be balanced against three positive aspects: a 50 percent reduction in water use (and cost), the option to mow or not to mow, and the fact that Buffalograss requires no fertilizer.

Though a homeowner's use of Buffalograss could result in significant savings of our basic water resource, equally significant savings could be had at golf courses, highway roadsides, parks and recreation areas, boulevards and so on.

The indiscriminate use and then necessary watering of Bluegrass in the Grow Native region borders on the insane. Until recent years Buffalograss could be grown only from seed, which had to be treated to assure quick germination. Now, however, Buffalograss sod is available, though only from a few growers. Also, now being offered are Buffalograss plugs, a considerably less costly method than sod. Buffalograss is stoloniferous, meaning it spreads by runners (like Creeping Bent, St. Augustine, and Bermuda grasses). The plugs are planted at 12-inch intervals and expected to spread into a solid turf. Both sod and plugs will respond to generous watering in order to secure fast growth and quick establishment of a solid turf.

A new and significant development is a method of replacing established Bluegrass lawn with Buffalograss. Obviously it is difficult to find anyone who would be enthusiastic about ripping up their beautiful Bluegrass lawn in order to plant Buffalograss, even though it can reduce their water bill by 50 percent and offer other benefits. However, the new method enables the owner to have his cake and eat it too.

Recent tests show that Buffalograss plugs will become established when planted in an established Bluegrass lawn with normal Bluegrass watering. Once the Buffalograss is established, the watering can be gradually reduced (by about 50 percent), the Bluegrass then gives way to the Buffalograss. The process does not occur in one season. Rather, depending on soil conditions, exposure, and so on, it requires patience and several seasons to fully develop.

HEIGHT—If left to grow it will attain a height of *3 to 6 inches.*

WATER—Requires *schedule #2, some watering,* for use as a lawn. If allowed to grow naturally, once established, Buffalograss can get by on schedule #1, little watering.

EXPOSURE—Withstands full exposure to wind. Grows best in full sun.

SUITABLE SUBSTITUTES—Two natives, *Bouteloua curtipendula,* Sideoats Grama, and *Bouteloua gracilis,* Blue Grama, may also be used as a short grass in natural situations, and both are better than Buffalograss above 7,500 feet.

Festuca ovina glauca
BLUE FESCUE
(FOREIGN)

The Blue Fescue has bristly, blue-gray foliage, which forms a rounded, moundlike tuft.

Its texture makes it useful for contrast.

SUGGESTED USES—You may use the Blue Fescue as a *ground cover in small grouped to mass plantings.* Because of its unique color it may also be used for *accent.*

PLANTING SPACE—Every *12 inches.*

HEIGHT—Attains a height of *6 to 12 inches.*

WATER—Requires *schedule #2, some watering,* and well-drained soil. Needs to be sheared back each spring to retain a good color.

EXPOSURE—Withstands exposure to wind. Grows well in either full sun or partial shade.

Cortaderia selloana
PAMPAS GRASS
(FOREIGN)

Pampas Grass has attractive, plumelike white spikes. These plumes may be cut and used for indoor decoration during the winter. With its plumes and gracefully arching leaves, Pampas Grass is probably the most impressive of the ornamental grasses.

SUGGESTED USES—You may use Pampas Grass individually or in *small grouped plantings* as a *specimen* or *accent*.

PLANTING SPACE—Every *4 to 6 feet*.

HEIGHT—Up to *10 feet*.

WATER—Requires *schedule #2, some watering*.

EXPOSURE—Withstands little exposure to wind. Grows best in full sun or partial shade and in a protected location as it is not especially hardy.

BASIC LANDSCAPE
DESIGN

The Design Process

In a general design sense it seems that the use of native materials is the thing to do. This includes plants. For instance, it somehow appears inappropriate to try to fit the classic white clapboard New England dwelling into the local semidesert region of the Rocky Mountains. The insensitivity of this relocation is too frequently compounded by the use of imported New England plant materials. The same inappropriateness similarly applies to the use of the typical flat-roofed stucco building of the arid desert Southwest. A design style with true western sensibility for this region is much desired for its utility of function and beauty.

The drawings on page 65 are examples of the landscape design process. Though these particular examples show a residential design, the process is basically the same for any kind of site development.

Drawing A is an existing conditions schematic study. As this step is the base for the final design it must be prepared carefully. It considers such features as: 1) major environmental influences—amount of sun, shade areas, and the direction of prevailing wind; 2) special use areas—relaxation, play, work, and private view; 3) site features—good and bad views to emphasize or obscure, slope of land, high and low areas, special soil conditions, existing plantings and structures (including details of the structure such as windows and doors), lot boundaries, and location of all utilities.

Once you have completed the existing conditions drawing, use it as a base map for planning your new landscape details. Don't sketch on it. Instead, lay a sheet of transparent paper over the existing base conditions and draw on the transparency. This procedure will enable you to change and redraw any number of times without losing the information on the base map.

Drawing B shows the final landscape design. In the case of this illustration we have not specifically named the plants as there will generally be more than one plant suitable for use in any given situation. We've indicated which type of plant to use—shade tree, evergreen tree, deciduous shrub, and so on.

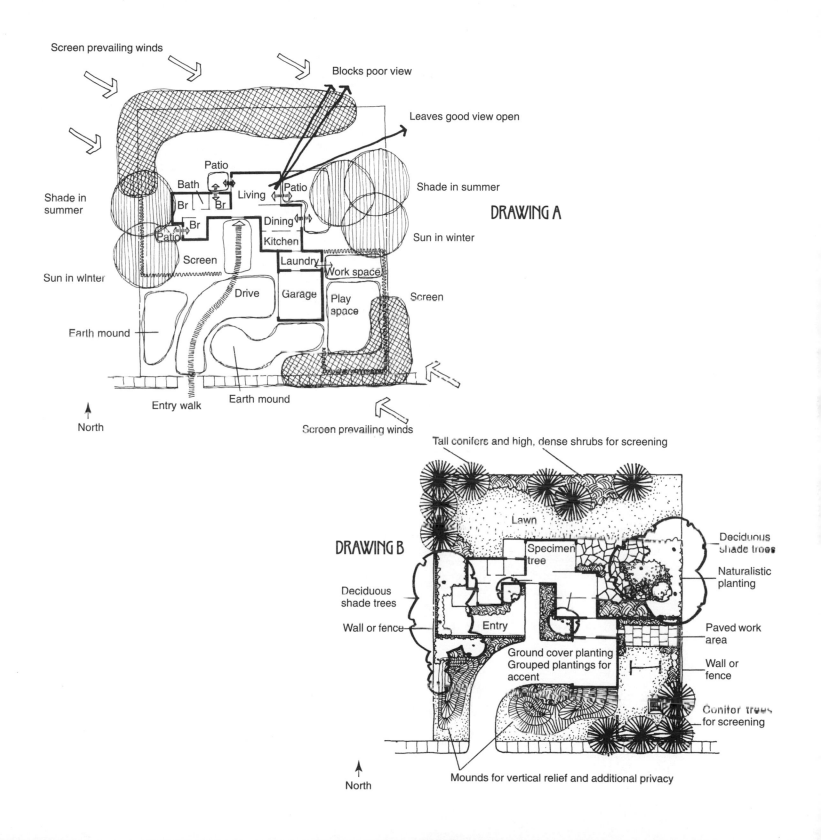

Screen prevailing winds

Blocks poor view

Leaves good view open

Shade in summer

DRAWING A

Patio

Bath

Br   Br   Living   Patio

Br

Patio   Dining

Screen   Kitchen

Shade in summer

Sun in winter

Laundry

Work space

Shade in summer

Sun in winter

Drive   Garage   Play space

Screen

Earth mound

Sun in winter

Earth mound

Entry walk

↑ North

Screen prevailing winds

Tall conifers and high, dense shrubs for screening

DRAWING B

Lawn

Specimen tree

Deciduous shade trees

Deciduous shade trees

Naturalistic planting

Wall or fence

Entry

Paved work area

Ground cover planting
Grouped plantings for accent

Wall or fence

Conifer trees for screening

Mounds for vertical relief and additional privacy

↑ North

Basic Design Styles

Each landscape design situation is different from the next because it is dependent on all the variable factors mentioned earlier, plus personal preferences. This variation makes it impossible to provide any hard and fast rules. There are, however, three fundamental design styles that we label "Random," "Curved Line," and "Straight Line." Most designs will be a combination of at least two, or possibly of all three styles.

RANDOM—The Random style is generally used for a full natural effect, or when almost complete freedom of line is desired. This does not mean that the landscape is haphazard. It is planned, but the result is a "casual" effect. This is the most difficult style to create and is best used as a transition area between a Curved Line or Straight Line and a bordering natural or wild area.

CURVED LINE—The Curved Line style is useful where a free-flowing but controlled effect is desired. It is neither as loose nor as natural as the Random style, nor as "engineered" or geometric as the Straight Line. It is the most satisfactory for most residential sites and it can be easily used in combination with either or both of the other styles.

STRAIGHT LINE—The Straight Line style is perhaps the easiest and most commonly used. This is because property boundaries are usually a series of straight lines, building outlines are usually straight, and streets are often laid out in grid patterns. However, a pure Straight Line design may prove to be too severe, too mechanical. It is usually improved by integrating the Curved Line style or Random style.

Orientation, proposed use, existing and future adjacent conditions, site features and ecology, and physical features of the land are a few of the factors that may influence the final design. There is usually more than one good design solution for a given site.

Design Considerations

Other design details that you might consider are "Grouping Plants by Water Requirements," "Massed Plantings vs. 'Shotgun' Plantings," "Foundation Plantings," and "Edgings."

GROUPING PLANTS BY WATER REQUIREMENTS—Plants used in grouped or mass plantings must have similar water requirements. If plants requiring little water are used in the same grouping with plants requiring much water, one or the other will suffer. They may die, grow rangy or misshapen, or become stunted. However, this factor will be avoided if a drip irrigation system is used (see page 76).

MASSED PLANTINGS VS. "SHOTGUN" PLANTINGS—One of the most common landscape errors is the scattered placement of plants without relation to one another—a tree here, a shrub over there, another over there. This type of planting gives a weak, confused, haphazard appearance to the landscape, aside from resulting in maintenance headaches, particularly the mowing of many small turf areas.

Where the planting areas are massed together—a tree here with a group of shrubs, another group of shrubs along with a nice pleasant open lawn area creates a stronger, unified, more organized appearance. This often can be done with the same number and kinds of plants or with slightly more plants. Even a specimen plant will generally benefit with a massed planting background. The lawn then becomes the foreground and is usable for games, play, and other outdoor activities.

FOUNDATION PLANTINGS—Many people tend to neglect the foundation planting as part of their landscape design. This element is very important for it provides a needed transition from the hard, vertical lines of a building to the softer, horizontal lines of the landscape. Also, it can serve to conceal any unsightly foundation tops.

Too often a foundation planting consists solely of an upright juniper on the corners with a couple of spreading junipers on either side. Much more can be achieved with the inclusion of a few deciduous types to provide a seasonal change and a softer line. Also, the walls of a building provide a good background for a specimen plant.

EDGINGS—Edgings, which are used to separate different surfaces, such as driveway and lawn or lawn and shrub border, not only save a great deal of maintenance time but they contribute more to a neat, clean appearance than any other element of a human-made landscape. The simplest and least expensive method of edging is an edge cut with a spade, but this takes a continuous effort to maintain. The five common edging materials are wood, steel, brick, concrete, and plastic. Use of these materials will ease the maintenance of flower beds and planting groups as well as strengthen the line of a design.

Wood, a natural material, blends very well with other landscape elements, but it is not permanent. Cedar and redwood are best because they are the longest lasting of the woods. As wood is very difficult to bend around curves, its use should be limited to straight runs. A more stable result will be achieved with a 2 x 4 than with any other size board. The wood edging should have a stake driven into the ground every 3 to 5 feet to hold it in place.

Steel edging has the advantage of permanence, and it can be easily used on curves. It is commercially available in black or green and a variety of 16- to 20-foot lengths. Trim roadways and walks or areas of crushed rock with 5 x $\frac{1}{4}$ edging. Trim paths and driveways with 4 x $\frac{3}{16}$ edging and planting areas, tree rings, and other light-duty applications with 4 x $\frac{1}{8}$ edging.

Brick, like wood, is a more natural material. When installed with care so that the lines are smooth and the top level, brick is a very attractive edging. It is very versatile and is particularly useful for an informal, rustic effect. However, it can be expensive. If not set in a permanent concrete foundation it will require occasional resetting. Some maintenance is necessary as grass will grow between the bricks, and it is more subject to frost action than the other materials.

Concrete edging is usually the most enduring of the edgings, but is the most expensive to install. It does not blend as well as wood or brick with the other landscape materials and is more suited to use on commercial rather than residential sites; however, it may be that a strong contrast is desired and if so, concrete edging serves this requirement.

Plastic, the heavier the better. It should be selected to resemble steel; however, it's usually too fragile and impermanent.

PLANTING INSTRUCTIONS

Bareroot Planting

By planting bareroot stock you may save a considerable amount of money over balled-and-burlapped or container stock. However, only deciduous trees and shrubs can be planted bareroot and even some deciduous trees and shrubs are exceptions to this rule and should be planted with a ball or from a container to assure a reasonable chance of success in the transplanting. Those that are planted bareroot will initially require some additional care.

The smaller the plant, the greater the chance of success in transplanting. Also, the odds of successful bareroot transplanting will increase in direct proportion to the amount of pruning of the top. As soon as the plant is in the ground and well watered, between a third and a half of the top should be judiciously cut off—not sheared but pruned to thin the plant, retaining its natural form.

Bareroot plants should be planted in early spring while they are still dormant. If it is impossible to plan to plant within a few days, the plants should be unwrapped and the roots "heeled in"—temporarily buried in a shallow trench and soaked—then planted.

Planting Instructions—Bareroot

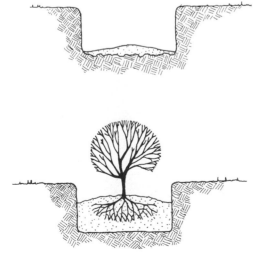

1. Protect roots against sun and wind before planting; keep damp.

2. Width and depth of hole are variable. Provide a minimum space of 6 inches from the ends of the roots in which to put the improved topsoil backfill.

3. Improved topsoil backfill: $\frac{1}{3}$ peatmoss and $\frac{2}{3}$ topsoil.

4. Sides straight.

5. Loosen hard subsoil in bottom of hole.

6. Mound bottom slightly and compact with improved topsoil backfill for proper drainage.

7. Set plant perpendicular and spread roots evenly and gently around mound before adding more improved topsoil backfill.

8. Set the plant in the soil to the same depth as grown at the nursery. The soil line found toward the bottom of the trunk will indicate

this. It is to that height that the soil, *not* the mulch, should come. Check with the nurseryperson to establish the correct height.

9. Work improved topsoil backfill around roots by hand.

10. Soak thoroughly until layers are completely saturated.

11. Add peat moss mulch as a "saucer" to help catch water.

12. Soak again.

13. Prune stems ⅓ to ½ their length.

Note: If roots have dried out, they should be soaked two hours before planting.

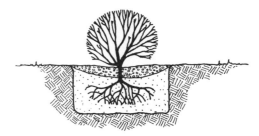

Container Planting

Most deciduous and evergreen broadleaf shrubs, deciduous trees, and many evergreen shrubs are sold in containers that range in size from 3-inch pots to bushel baskets. Though container stock is more expensive than bareroot, the shock of transplanting is reduced and the chances of survival greatly increased. The planting season of container stock is much longer than with bareroot stock; in fact, many plants can be planted throughout the year. Your nurseryperson can tell you the optimum time to plant individual varieties.

Planting Instructions—Container and Balled-and-Burlapped

1. Width and depth of hole are variable. Provide the container or ball (except for pines and upright junipers, see below) a minimum space of 6 inches for a cushion of improved topsoil backfill.

2. Improved topsoil backfill: ⅓ peatmoss and ⅔ topsoil.

3. Sides straight.

4. Loosen hard subsoil in bottom of hole.

5. Mound bottom slightly and compact with improved topsoil backfill for proper drainage.

6. Set top of container or ball flush with the existing ground level. Plant should be set perpendicular before back-filling.

7. If in a container, cut container and remove plant. (If the container soil is hard and dry and appears not easily broken, then the container may be removed before the plant is placed in the hole.) If balled-and-burlapped, loosen burlap around the top, but leave otherwise intact. Be very careful not to break the ball.

8. Work improved topsoil carefully around ball and soak thoroughly for proper compaction.

9. Add peat moss mulch as a "saucer" to help catch water.

Note: All trees over 4 feet tall should be staked and guyed for the first year.

Balled-and-Burlapped Planting (Pines and Upright Junipers)

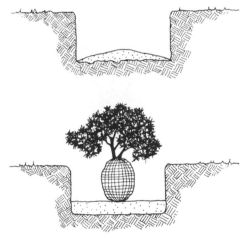

Large deciduous trees, many evergreen shrubs, and most evergreen trees are sold balled-and-burlapped. The stock is dug with a ball of dirt around the roots and the ball is then wrapped with burlap and tied up with cord or string. With the exception of pines and upright junipers, "B&B" stock is planted in the same manner as container stock (see page 71).

Planting Instructions—Balled-and-Burlapped (Pines and Upright Junipers)

The planting method for pines and upright junipers is the same as that specified for container and balled-and-burlapped except that instead of being set level or slightly below the groundline the root ball is set slightly higher (about 4 inches) and mounded. This ensures the additional drainage that these plants require.

Staking and Guying Trees

Initial Plant Protection

Deciduous trees (8 feet or taller), evergreen trees (3½ feet or taller), and large shrubs should always be staked and guyed for at least the first year, or until a good, secure root system has been established. Otherwise they may be uprooted by the wind or tilted before they can settle. There are several methods of staking, the best of which is shown.

Instructions—Staking and Guying Trees

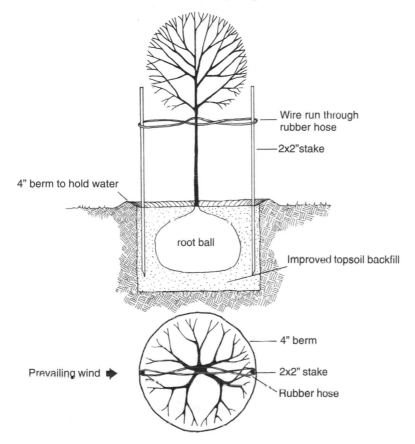

Trees with thin bark are susceptible to winter burn and should have their trunks (and major branches, if any) wrapped with burlap or paper wrapping for at least the first year. This wrapping material can be purchased at most garden shops. Check with your nurseryperson for instructions.

We wish to mention again that when watering, a good thorough soaking is much more effective and efficient than frequent, light sprinklings that only moisten the soil a couple of inches. This is particularly true immediately following planting.

WATERING SCHEDULE

Note: When planting, thoroughly soak the backfill in the planting hole.

Schedule #1, little watering
> 1st year. Soak every two weeks
> 2nd year. Soak every three weeks
> 3rd year. Soak once a month
> 4th year on. Water only during extended dry periods

Schedule #2, some watering
> 1st year. Soak every week
> 2nd year. Soak every two weeks
> 3rd year on. Soak every three to four weeks

Schedule #3, much watering
> 1st year. Soak twice a week
> 2nd year. Soak once a week
> 3rd year on. Soak every two weeks

A great improvement over the sprinkler system that waters everything—lawn, trees, and shrubs—indiscriminately and equally is the *drip system.* A drip system is simply a water line with bubbler heads. It can, for instance, be laced through a shrub border with the bubblers plugged in only at each shrub so that the bubblers are tailored to the water requirements of that particular plant area. Such drip lines can be extended to amazing lengths because they require little water pressure—as compared to the sprinkler system, which requires high pressure to create the necessary spray. Drip lines are inexpensive relative to sprinkler lines as they need not be buried but will function normally if covered with only a light mulch. Bubbler heads are easily moved around to increase or decrease water at individual plants. As native plants become established and water needs reduced, bubblers may be removed.

The drip system is a great conservator of water and is ideal for the landscape with a Bluegrass lawn and native trees and shrubs in conjunction. Also, the drip system is ideal for the Buffalograss and all native plants landscape. The combination of sprinkler and drip systems serves to establish the plants, then uses the appropriate watering schedule to ensure indefinite growth and beauty.

The optimum time for watering is early morning. If this isn't possible, then water in the evening, although consistently watering at that time may result in mildew or other fungi. In our dry climate this shouldn't be much of a problem though. As a rule, late morning or afternoon watering is less effective because much water will be lost to evaporation.

Whenever you water, we strongly recommend long soakings or long sprinklings as opposed to frequent, light soakings or sprinklings. Long soakings are much more effective in that they result in healthier plants. Long soakings create moisture reserves in the soil and, more importantly, plants can develop stronger, deeper-reaching root systems. This is especially true during the period immediately after planting. Low-volume sprinklings that only moisten the top few inches of soil create little or no moisture reserve and encourage a shallow root system that cannot withstand long periods between waterings.

AFTERWORD

We hope we have not given the impression that the natives are oddballs suitable only to be placed on display as curiosities. Rather, we hope we have conveyed the feeling that the natives are to be preferred over foreigners for the cultured landscapes of the foothills region. With some exceptions, a native can be found to fulfill most landscape design needs, be it a large tree for shade, a smaller tree for flower and fruit, a shrub for a barrier or screen, or a grass for the lawn. The need that cannot be fulfilled by natives is for floral displays of horiculturally developed, highly exotic plants such as the cultured roses, annuals, perennials, bulbs, and tubers. Actually, as these displays generally occupy only a small part of the landscape, the foliage background and turf can just as well consist of natives.

QUICK REFERENCE CHART TO NATIVE PLANTS

	Plant	American Plum	Barrel, Pincushion, and Prickly Pear Cacti	Blue Avena	Blue Fescue	Bristlecone Pine	Buffalograss	Bush Cinquefoil	Clematis	Colorado Blue Spruce	Colorado Pinyon Pine	Colorado Redosier Dogwood	Common Hackberry	Creeping Mahonia	Curl-leaf Mountain Mahogany	Douglas Fir	Fleshy Hawthorn	Gambel Oak	Giant Reed	Golden Currant	Indigobush Amorpha	Kinnikinnick
Page		9	49	57	60	17	58–59	28	48	16	18	26	2	51	40	20	3	31	56	34	23	46
Water	Water Schedule #1, little		●								●				●					●		
	Water Schedule #2, some	●		●	●	●	●	●	●				●	●		●		●				●
	Water Schedule #3, much									●		●					●		●		●	
Type	Large Tree (30'–100')					●				●			●			●						
	Small Tree (10'–30')	●									●						●	●				
	Shrub	●						●				●			●			●		●	●	
	Ground Cover		●	●	●		●		●					●					●			●
Features	Deciduous	●						●	●			●	●				●	●		●	●	
	Evergreen					●				●	●			●	●	●						●
	Flower	●	●	●				●	●			●		●	●		●		●	●	●	●
	Fruit-seed	●	●	●					●			●		●	●		●	●		●	●	●
	Foliage		●	●	●	●	●			●	●			●	●	●	●	●	●		●	●
	Bark	●				●						●										
	Form		●	●	●				●						●		●	●	●			
Tolerances	Drought Resistant		●				●		●		●		●	●	●	●				●		
	Alkaline Soil Tolerant												●								●	
	Full Exposure to Wind		●		●	●	●	●	●		●		●				●	●				
	Full Sun	●	●	●	●	●	●	●	●	●	●	●	●	●	●	●	●	●	●	●	●	●
	Partial Shade	●		●	●		●	●	●	●		●	●	●		●	●	●	●			●
	Full Shade	●						●		●			●	●		●						●
Uses	Barrier Planting		●																			
	Plant Screen	●									●	●			●	●		●		●		
	Shade Tree	●				●				●			●			●		●				
	Accent	●		●	●			●		●	●	●		●		●	●		●			●
	Specimen	●	●	●		●		●		●	●	●			●	●	●	●	●			
	Small Grouped Planting		●	●	●			●	●						●			●	●	●		
	Large Grouped Planting	●	●		●			●	●							●		●		●	●	
	Mass Planting	●			●				●											●	●	
	Ground Cover				●		●	●	●					●								●

Plant	Page
Lamb's Ear	52
Montmorency Cherry	10
Mountain Common Juniper	41
Mountain Ninebark	27
Mugho Swiss Mountain Pine	43
Narrowleaf Poplar	6
One-seed Juniper	14
Oregon Grape	42
Pampas Grass	61
Peachleaf Willow	11
Plains Poplar	7
Ponderosa Pine	19
Pussytoes	47
Quaking Aspen	8
Rocky Mountain Juniper	15
Rocky Mountain Maple	22
Rocky Mountain Smooth Sumac	32
Russian Olive	4
Sagebrush	24
Small Soapweed	53
Thimbleberry	37
Three-leaf Sumac	33
True Mountain Mahogany	25
Western Chokecherry	30
Western Sand Cherry	29
Whitestem Gooseberry	35
Wild Rose	36
Wild Strawberry	50
Yellow Transparent Apple	5

ABOUT THE AUTHORS

S. Huddleston

S. Huddleston is a noted professional planner and landscape architect. He is a Fellow Emeritus of the American Society of Landscape Architects and a member of the American Institute of Planners. Now retired, he headquartered in Denver and practiced throughout the West, even as far afield as Alaska. Sam's abiding, lifelong interest in outdoor activities and the environment shows itself in the kinds of projects his firm has worked on—from the 22,000-acre Franklin Mountains Wilderness Park for the city of El Paso, Texas, to comprehensive long-range plans for numerous counties and towns in Colorado.

He believes that "man has no alternative but to work harder to adjust his lifestyle to the environment, rather than vice versa; and the use of appropriate plants is an important key to more efficient land use and utilization of resources. Landscaping with native plants, including buffalograss, helps mitigate one of our more serious transgressions on the environment—our excessive use of water, about half of which goes to maintain foreign plants and lawns."

M. Hussey grew up in Iowa, but many of his childhood summers were spent in Colorado with his geologist father. He developed a love for the area and after a stint with the army in Augsburg, Germany, headed to Colorado where he started a career as a landscape architect with the Huddleston firm.